GHOSTS OF THE JERSEY SHORE II

GHOSTS OF THE JERSEY SHORE II

LYNDA LEE MACKEN

GHOSTS OF THE JERSEY SHORE II

Published by: Black Cat Press
P. O. Box 1218
Forked River, NJ 08731
www.lyndaleemacken.com

Photo Credits: Library of Congress title page, pages x, 4, 7, 14, 34, 36, 37, 40, 58, 59, 60, 62 and 76; Wikimedia Commons page 5 and 16; Jason Meehan pages 9, 10, 11 and 12; Shannon Abello page 20; Jim Kudrick pages 23 and 25; Shutterstock page 51 and 53; the Atlantic County Court House photo by Tim Kiser on page 72 is licensed under the Creative Commons ShareAlike 2.5 Generic license; Seaville Tavern patron page 84; all other photographs by author.

Although the author/publisher make every effort to ensure the accuracy and completeness of information contained in this book, we assume no responsibility for errors, inaccuracies, omission or any inconsistency herein. Any slights of people, places or organizations are unintentional. For information, please contact Black Cat Press.

ISBN 978-0-9829580-3-2

Printed in the United States of America by Sheridan Books, Inc.
www.sheridan.com

Book Layout & Cover Design by Deb Tremper,
Six Penny Graphics.
www.sixpennygraphics.com

In the universe,
there are things that are known,
and things that are unknown,
and in between, there are doors.
~ William Blake

CONTENTS

"All dimensions are in the same location."
~ Hans Bender, Parapsychologist

INTRODUCTION

For the ghosts of the Jersey Shore it's just another day at the beach but for those of us who are entranced by their presence, it's *so* much more. From ghosts and ghouls, phantoms and poltergeists, to eerie haunted houses rife with shadows we remain captivated by the uncanny and the unexplained. Earthbound souls continue to vex us wherever they stay tethered.

Fear of the unknown is the chill factor in every ghost story. Does life continue after death? The spirits who haunt us seem to inhabit an environment intersecting our own. Do ghosts exist in alternate realms and somehow slip into our reality? In 1954, Hugh Everett III, a Princeton University student, pronounced parallel universes exist. Where and how these spaces occur remains a mystery.

For 22 years, the late psychic Alex Tanous served as the American Society of Psychical Research's leading "gifted" subject in many experiments. Tanous believed ghosts exist because they need to tell their story in order to achieve balance. Despite his extensive knowledge of the spirit world, he too puzzled over why ghosts appear. In *Conversations with Ghosts* he says, "They vary widely, some are perceived as an unrecognizable mist, others are so lifelike they are almost, or often, mistaken for real people. Some behave as though they are re-enacting shadows of tragic events from the past; others are only in the here-and-now and related directly to observers." He explains that spirits are in some way earthbound energy.

Everything in this world, even the tiniest grain of beach sand, consists of energy. Simply put, energy is information that moves or vibrates. The energy of a table or a chair moves slowly therefore these objects can be seen and touched proving they exist. However, most energy in this world can't be seen, touched or heard with our five senses—like electricity, for instance, yet we know electricity exists. It moves so fast we can't perceive the energy but we notice its effects.

The human body emanates energy that is imprinted on physical locales, structures and even objects. Since energy cannot be destroyed it's theorized the energy emitted during a lifetime somehow embeds itself on the environment. That explains why some antiques or other belongings can be "possessed." We all possess psychic abilities but some humans have an extraordinary sensory perception. These individuals can perceive the residual energy left behind by those who once occupied places and they can also "read" the energy in articles once owned by those deceased to obtain information. The clairvoyantly acquired material can be researched through official records to help confirm the identity of the resident spirit. Psychics are invaluable in explaining paranormal phenomenon yet there are those who doubt psychic ability; a defensible viewpoint when one psychic offers information but when three or four or more suggest similar scenarios, well, that's evidence.

Ghost hunting is the process of investigating haunted locations. These paranormal investigators collect evidence in support of supernatural activity by utilizing a variety of electronic equipment. Electromagnetic field (EMF) detectors and digital thermometers detect energy fluctuations and infrared cameras detect variations in heat versus light so they display a lower-energy frequency wavelength emitted by an invisible to the naked eye form. (It's all about energy!) Audio recorders can capture electronic voice phenomena (EVP) an occurrence whereby a spirit communicates to questions posed by the investigator. These are just a few tools of the ghost hunter's trade.

Our coastal, or should I say "ghost"al, heritage enjoys a wealth of spooky stories spanning centuries. The specters of Native Americans, soldiers, nurses, nannies and everyday folk are among the spirits who collide with seaside residents and visitors leaving disquieting feelings and frayed nerves in their wake. For those of us fascinated by the paranormal, we fancy them for their continued presence. The wide strand of landmarks, homes, hotels and restaurants spirited by the energy of those who lived before are brought back to life, so to speak, by the psychics and paranormal investigators who help explain the hauntings produced by ghostly presences.

After 15 years of chronicling ghost stories I find the prevalence of paranormal activity at historic villages astonishing. The Jersey Shore's Historic Allaire Village, Batsto Village and Historic Cold Spring Village do not disappoint. History plays a hand in the ghostly goings on but I believe bucolic settings are an additional factor. Ghosts were once people and, like all of us, they are social creatures drawn to peaceful places. Living history villages are idyllic oasis for visitors on both sides of the veil.

The coastal plain of the mysterious Pine Barrens, where indigenous pygmy trees remain an unexplainable natural phenomenon, are haunted by atmospheric ghost lights or "pine lights," in this case. They manifest at night over bogs, marshes and swamps appearing as eerie will-o'-the-wisp glows of phosphorescent light. The mysterious one million acre Pinelands also gave rise to the lore of the Jersey Devil. There are many versions of the 19th century legend concerning a certain Mrs. Leeds who found herself pregnant with a 13th child. In a fit of rage over her plight, she allegedly hoped it would be a devil. Mrs. Leeds received her wish when the child was born a demon! The wretched babe gave a screech, unfolded its wings and flew out the nursery window into the swamps. The Pine Barrens is also home to other creepy creations such as the former Royal Pines Hotel in Bayville where haunting rumors linger about the brooding structure.

The lure of the sea initially attracted visitors to Atlantic City—one of the state's first tourist destinations. The glitzy resort hardly conjures a haunted aura but some guests at Resorts Casino Hotel feel otherwise. The gambling house holds a considerable history and several ghost stories complement the past. But the big bizarre story in Atlantic County concerns the ghostly goings on in the 1838 county courthouse. The old court confines numerous sprits that make strange noises and even throw things!

Cape May is a haunted metropolis. In 1766, Cape Island, as then known, developed as a place where many journeyed for health and pleasure. Tourists first arrived from Philadelphia by horse-drawn wagons, stagecoaches, sloops and schooners. They lodged in rustic public houses and resident homes. There are literally dozens of haunted places in the Victorian city-by-the-sea—many of the spirits who remain originally stayed as summer guests. In this volume we visit the many ghosts haunting the Cape May Fish Market, Cape May Puffin Suites, and my "namesake," The Linda Lee.

Do spirits offer us a glimpse into the world beyond? Do parallel dimensions seep into one another? At this point in time we can only speculate. Let's leave these grave questions behind and embark on an eerie journey along the haunted Jersey Shore…

ASBURY PARK

PARANORMAL MUSEUM

We start our supernatural sojourn in the seaside
community of Asbury Park developed in the late
19th century by businessman James A. Bradley. The
visionary installed a boardwalk, orchestra pavilion
and pier along the waterfront followed by Ernest
Schnitzler who in 1888 built the once famous but
now extinct Palace Merry-Go-Round. During these
early decades a number of grand hotels went up
to accommodate the half million vacationers. The
country-by-the-sea's downtown area flourished
during this period and well into the 20th century.

Tourist travel began to flounder with the opening
of the (haunted) Garden State Parkway in 1947.
Fewer vacationers took trains to the seashore. Area
malls and office parks that opened in the 1960s
sounded the death knell for AP's downtown business
and aging boardwalk amusements couldn't compete

with area theme parks. Riots broke out in the 70s and by the 80s and 90s streets stood virtually empty.

The good news is, like the phoenix, Asbury rose from the ashes! The once-dilapidated inner city reemerged and Paranormal Books & Curiosities on Cookman Avenue is one reflection of the city's revival. Owned and operated by Kathy Kelly, the author and paranormal researcher opened the bookstore on Friday the 13th in June 2008. The attractive shop brims with books on every spooky subject alongside ghost hunting equipment and other paranormal products. The shop also offers psychic readings, séances, tours and workshops among other related events including opportunities to investigate haunted places.

One year later, Kelly opened the Paranormal
Museum adjacent to the book and curiosity shop.
That's when things got scary. The storefront gallery
showcases historical and educational artifacts
exploring unexplained mysteries like the Jersey
Devil, for instance. To quote Kelly, the museum is
"jam packed with strange relics and uniquities from
around the world."

In order to meet the opening deadline, an
exhibition artist worked alone installing the Jersey

Devil display in the middle of the night. Much to his dismay the craftsman saw "something" running around inside the space. He immediately exited the building and from then on only worked during daylight hours. Kelly is a diehard skeptic so she took the worker's story with a grain of salt. However, months later as she worked solo in her office *she* heard what sounded like someone running around the museum. She shrugged it off until someone laughed so close to her ear she jumped! Kelly departed straightaway.

Over time, others, including this writer, perceived a child-like presence in the hallway between the museum and the shop. Being the consummate investigator, Kelly left an audio recorder on overnight in the museum. The next morning over 70 minutes of sound was recorded on the device (!), mostly hammering and *running* noises. Still not convinced, the proprietor left the recorder on in her office overnight and before leaving explained out loud to the invisible entity that she didn't want it to leave—she wanted to know its identity. The next day during play back, listeners can hear Kelly leaving the office, shutting the door and then a child's voice clearly say, "Bye!"

In her book *Asbury Park's Ghosts and Legends*, Kelly relates dozens of sightings and reports of being touched. Best of all, although not to the recipient, is one person claimed someone hugged her legs. The off putting experience caused her to misstep and break a foot bone.

Recently a young boy proceeded through the museum and claimed he noticed the reflection of another child behind him when looking through the glass at Alice the doll. The boy believed the reflection was his sister's. Then he saw Alice blink. Kelly recounts in her *Nightmare at the Museum* blog, "He wasn't frightened but a little confused since he noted his sister had not entered the museum (I know this to be a fact)… I found him to be very genuine."

PARAMOUNT THEATER

On September 8, 1934, the *SS Morro Castle* steamed north from her weekly port o'call to Havana. Her captain suffered a fatal heart attack en route. To make matters worse, at 3:00 AM, fire broke out in a closet and quickly accelerated only hours before docking in New York harbor. A nor'easter drove the disabled vessel closer to shore as desperate passengers and crew tried to escape the flames. The few lifeboats launched carried mostly crew members to safety.

Unable to sail under her own power, a Coast Guard cutter eventually attempted to tow the damaged ship to its final destination. Tumultuous seas snapped the tow lines and the burning hulk came to rest on a sandbar in front of Asbury Park's Convention Hall.

The hull still smoldered the following morning when inspectors boarded the ship in search of victims and valuables. The massive fire consumed the decks and gutted the cabins—all 137 crew and passengers perished. Corpses were laid out on the Paramount Theatre stage for identification purposes. For a small fee, interested ghouls could gawk at the cadavers. Thousands of curious spectators and reporters lined the boardwalk to see the charred remains.

The *Morro Castle* remained on the sandbar for many months and spurred an economic boom for the city since suffering the effects of the Great Depression. City officials capitalized on the event and turned the wreck into a tourist attraction by charging $5 to ride the breeches buoy onto the deck. On March 14, 1935, the ruined *Morro Castle* finally ended up in New York's Gravesend Bay for scrap.

Coincidentally, at almost the identical location off Asbury Park, the immigrant ship *New Era* wrecked in dense fog on November 13, 1854.

Asbury Park's Paramount Theatre is co-located

with Convention Hall on the boardwalk. The completion of the third Madison Square Garden in New York
and Atlantic City's new Convention Center put city
officials under pressure to construct a similar venue
for Asbury Park. In 1927, a mysterious fire destroyed
the 5th Avenue Arcade on the boardwalk. Shortly
thereafter, a referendum passed to construct a conference center on the plot. The architectural design
included a 1600-seat theatre and a 3200-seat convention hall connected by an enclosed grand concourse.

Walter Reade, who already owned four theatres
in Asbury Park, received a contract to book movies
at the venue. Since he brokered with the Paramount

film distributor he named the showplace the Paramount Theatre. On New Year's Day, 1930, the film *Wings* inaugurated the new cinema which featured a mix of movies and live performances. A more spectacular grand opening followed on July 11, 1930, attended by Hollywood luminaries Ginger Rogers, Ed Wynn, Fredric March, Carole Lombard and the Marx Brothers.

When Garden State Ghost Hunters (GSGHS) investigated the infamous theatre, every team member heard inexplicable footfalls, knocking noises and ethereal voices. A few felt phantom touches. Crew member Tina Bates experienced an unseen entity pull one of her earrings off and several witnesses watched it sail across the room. The group discerned shadow people on stage and one of their thermo cameras picked up the heat signature of human buttocks on one of the seats in the theater! Team members scrambled when a light bulb flew off a shelf four feet away in response to their question, "Are you unhappy with us being here?" Are these fuming entities leftover energies from the awful *Morro Castle* disaster? Are the incorporeal beings present here resentful over their untimely death on a pleasure cruise coupled with the further insult of morbid opportunists profiting from their death?

Several psychics sensed a fire once raged

through the performers' dressing rooms and indeed singe marks are still evident on the walls. Sadly, no emergency exit door regulations existed at the time so the entertainers became trapped and perished in the flames. When psychic medium Barbara Lee first visited the location, she received an immediate rush of information regarding the catastrophe as opposed to her usual process of receiving fleeting images. The space is unusually charged with a thick, heavy energy. In fact, Lee detected spirits gasping for air— hardly able to breathe, the empath perceived people suffocating from smoke inhalation.

When GSGHS captured evidence of a human form with their infrared equipment they forwarded the video to Syfy channel's *Fact or Faked, Paranormal Files*. The program follows a team of investigators, led by a former FBI agent, who reviews various photographs and videos of alleged paranormal activity. If a particular piece of evidence warrants further investigation, the team sets out to recreate and explain the sighting. In this case, specialists recreated the anomaly but determined GSGHS' choice of equipment was erroneous. However, when *Fact of Faked* cast members performed their own investigation of the historic theatre they corroborated many of GSGHS' above mentioned findings thereby authenticating paranormal activity at the Paramount.

WALL TOWNSHIP

MARCONI HOTEL

Radio inventor Guglielmo Marconi established his American Wireless Telegraph Company headquarters near the banks of the Shark River in 1914. Although designated the "Belmar Station," the installation was actually located in Wall Township. Marconi provided a 2 ½ story brick hotel for unmarried employees. The building included a restaurant supplied with fresh vegetables grown on-site.

With the outbreak of World War I, Marconi's peaceful enterprise short-circuited when the U.S. Navy appropriated the communication operation at the Belmar Station. After the war, Marconi resumed control of his enterprise that eventually led to the development of the Radio Corporation of America (RCA). After a decade, Marconi established an office in New York City and left the Belmar Station.

    The Ku Klux Klan under the pseudonym "The Pleasure Seekers Association" occupied the property in the 1920s. By that time a great number of immigrants from New York and North Jersey summered at the Jersey Shore. Their influx generated an anti-immigrant movement attracting the attention of the Klan whose ultimate goal became the reclamation of coastal resorts from refugee tourists. Eventually political pressure forced the KKK to vacate Wall Township. Many years later an evangelical, liberal arts institution operated at the location.

    The 90-acre site stood empty until the U.S. Army took over the property in 1941. As an annex of Fort Monmouth, the U.S. Signal Corps set up shop as

Camp Evans, named after another radio pioneer, Lieutenant Colonel Paul W. Evans.

Experimentation with electronic echo techniques achieved its zenith with "Project Diana" on January 10, 1946. Pioneering scientists and engineers "bounced" the first radar signal off the moon and back in two and a half seconds. The project, named for the moon goddess, helped birth the National Aeronautics Space Administration (NASA).

Today the former top secret military installation is home to InfoAge. Part of the non-profit organization's mission is the historic preservation of the Marconi station and the World War II radar laboratory buildings. In addition, the location is also home to the New Jersey Antique Radio Club and the National Broadcasters Hall of Fame.

Over the years, tales of murder and mayhem have swirled about the site. Speculation abounds about alien infiltration, underground tunnels and war prisoner abuse at the former military base. Could these mysterious intrigues be the cause of the unexplained occurring at the former Marconi Hotel?

Some of InfoAge's Board members, volunteers and even visitors claim to see indistinct apparitions, experience unusual events and suffer inexplicable feelings. Shadow figures lurk about the historic hotel building and the feeling of being watched is unnerving. Strange noises and incorporeal whispers are chilling along with disembodied screams, howls, moans, ghostly music and singing. This is one extremely haunted location!

The Leni Lenape once thrived at the location. Do Native American spirits still seethe over losing their land? Are the perceived shadow people Nazi spies' spirits? During World War II Colonel Paul Watson died in the Marconi Hotel. Is his spirit still in residence? When it comes to ghosts and hauntings many questions go unanswered but with recent advances in technology some mysteries are becoming solvable.

The Behind the Wall (BTW) Paranormal organization regularly conducts investigations of the site using a wide-range of technology. Night vision capabilities help capture events in darkened rooms and the infrared cameras catch anomalies not apparent to the naked eye. By utilizing flashlights and K2 meters the group asked specific questions of the unseen entities instructing the spirits to flash the lights in a certain way in response. As a result they determined the presences inside the building consisted of both genders, adults and children, along with Native Americans and military personnel. Some of the entities responded positively via the light flashes when asked if they were frightened, hiding or angry. Strong emotions can bond spirits to a location.

The paranormal research group even obtained several instances of electronic voice phenomenon (EVP). On one audio clip a male voice clearly states he's "jealous" in response to why he stays behind. Numerous EVP evidence led the group to conclude animal spirits (dogs barking, howling) still haunt the area. Other EVP evidence includes the command to "get out!" In response to a researcher asking what happened to them, "Murder, murder!" was the eerie reply. When one of the ghost hunters asked a fellow crew member to hold his camera an unseen entity is audibly heard on playback saying "I'll smash that camera in your eye." Occasionally the investigators hear actual, audible, yet indecipherable, voices.

In the able hands of the BTW paranormal research group 35mm cameras obtained photographic evidence. Several snapshots contained odd-colored mists and other unusual colors superimposed over members' skin. In one photo a black handprint appeared over a member's eye. Most dramatically, one picture showed a figure peeking out the door and another revealed a form standing in a doorway.

When called in for a paranormal assist at Camp Evans, Boni Bates and Garden State Ghost Hunters discerned the presence of Native Americans and identified their burial ground. Bates observed numerous shadow people, as did others, at the Marconi Hotel. The spirit of an older gent, possibly military, stood proud and seemed to be standing watch in the military museum. She detected two

men in the ballroom and in the attic she discerned
a wounded black man hiding from the KKK. Bates
feels the spirits of several Germans, both prisoners
and scientists, on the property. All these perceptions
fall in line with the site's long history.

BTW manager, Gloria Karduk, felt something
touch her head and face in the second floor conference
room. While investigating she felt persistently yet
gently pushed until she fell onto a bench. In a photo
taken at the time there is a black mark on her pants at
the exact spot where she felt the shove.

BTW offers opportunities to conduct
personal paranormal investigations at the very
haunted Marconi Hotel. Contact BTW at www.
behindthewallparanormal.com for information.

SPRING LAKE

WHITE LILAC INN

Spring Lake became a fashionable seaside resort in the early 1900s. The town boasted fine hotels, lavish estates and pretentious private homes known as "cottages" which surrounded a beautiful clear spring-fed pond named "Spring Lake."

Nearly 20% of America's inns are designated haunted spots and that's a good thing for over 60% of guests prefer to stay at haunted lodgings. Spring Lake's White Lilac Inn offers ample opportunity to sleep with a ghost for those open to the other world. The historic home at 414 Central Avenue possesses a friendly spirit who simply does not want to leave the house she once called home.

Former owner Sally Mann Randock Francis enjoyed wearing floral scented perfume and often wore fresh flower corsages. Every now and then guests at the White Lilac Inn remark they detect a flowery fragrance on the staircase. The phenomena is always noticed at the same spot. It's presumed the sweet aroma is Sally's signature scent announcing her ethereal presence descending the stairs to keep an eye on things.

Thrice-married, Sally worked as a New York model in the 1940s. She possessed a passion for entertaining guests in her Spring Lake home and even welcomed the Ziegfeld Follies' girls. Given the colorful nature of the model's lifestyle, it is believed her presence lingers to insure guests enjoy their stay as much as she enjoyed attending to visitors in her day.

Spirits seem to enjoy the comfort of a bed and breakfast inn as living guests do but there is no need to fear here. Francis is a subtle spirit who radiates a positive energy—a little something extra that often prompts guests to comment about the good aura they sense about the inn.

FARMINGDALE

HISTORIC ALLAIRE VILLAGE

Howell Works was a bog-iron production facility for pig iron established in the early 19th century. In 1822, Allaire purchased the iron works as a resource for his Allaire Iron Works in New York City. At the time, his company led the manufacture of marine steam engines. He cast the brass air chamber for Robert Fulton's *Clermont* and sailed with Fulton on the steamboat's historic maiden voyage. The Howell Works also manufactured cast iron products. Allaire eventually transformed the Howell Works into a self-sufficient community, complete with housing and food supply for the workforce and its own post office, church, school and company store. The town even issued its own currency.

Bog iron production became obsolete by the increasing availability of iron ore so in 1846, the

Howell Works furnace was extinguished. Allaire continued living in his village, maintaining his New York works, until his death in 1858. When he died, the town's name changed to Allaire, New Jersey.

Today's Historic Allaire Village is a notable example of an early American company town. The village is also noteworthy for its ghostly inhabitants. In the Visitors Center for instance, psychics detect a strong, male energy. The entity is described as a nasty, angry man in boots. Village history records Benjamin Marks as the village supervisor who lived in one of the early row houses which were rebuilt on the original foundation. Marks disliked his job according to psychics who are able to read his energy. One morning as staffers performed their routine security check in the cellar they heard the sound of heavy footfalls. They cautiously approached the interloper and encountered the partial apparition of a man wearing boots! They suspect this startling effect was a postmortem visit from the tyrannical manager. Other mystifying manifestations in the building are electrical anomalies—lights, projectors, cameras and security systems usually go haywire for no reason.

Eric Mabius is an actor whose father became the museum director at Historic Allaire Village in the 1980s. The Mabius family lived on site and Eric and his brother considered the 330 acre park their playground. One foggy night they approached the "Big House," the founder's former residence. Dim security lights illumined the empty house as Mabius peered through the window in response to the sound of inconsolable sobbing he heard coming from inside. He observed a tall figure dressed in funeral garb including a top hat. The man didn't seem "right," Mabius said. The apparition appeared heartbroken and turned his head toward Mabius and looked him in the eye. The sighting terrified the actor and troubled him for years.

Psychic medium Kim Russo hosts the documentary television series *The Haunting of…* In 2012, Eric Mabius appeared on the program in an effort to obtain an explanation for his disturbing experience.

When a cholera epidemic hit New York City in 1832, James Allaire moved his family out of the city to his Howell village but to no avail. His wife, Frances, died of the disease and Russo received the vision of a woman dying in an upstairs bedroom.

Russo also discerned the bodies of other cholera victims buried on the grounds particularly in the open quad area between the General Store and Allaire's mansion. For years the story of a lady in white floating over the area persisted at this location on the property. Psychics say the white lady was an ardent admirer of Hal Allaire, the founder's son, even though she was bequeathed to a sailor. Her mariner never returned so they say she stays behind awaiting her beloved—or maybe to catch Hal's attention.

The death of his wife triggered a downward spiral for James Allaire. Shortly thereafter, a ship in which Allaire was part-owner, the *William Gibbons*, ran aground and wrecked. During that same year, the Howell Works furnace blew and production temporarily ceased. The following year, America plunged into a severe recession and Allaire's uninsured steamboat *Home,* sank with the loss of 100 lives. The catastrophe damaged Allaire's reputation and practically wiped him out financially.

Another ghost in residence is Hal Allaire. He also haunts the Big House and his playful spirit enjoys taunting the costumed interpreters who work in the house. Hal lived at Allaire as a virtual recluse until his death in 1901. Without the funds to maintain the site the buildings fell into disrepair. The property became known as the Deserted Village of Allaire. The otherworldly Hal likes to move books and household objects and apparently possesses a fondness for playing with candles. This proclivity became obvious when Russo, who discerned Hal's presence along with his father's, posed questions to the men. The lighted candle on the table responded quite animatedly during the show.

Allaire Village is an epicenter of ghostly and paranormal activity. The village offers a spooky hayride, a haunted mansion, ghost stories, paranormal experts and tarot card readings around Halloween. All events are family friendly and not too scary. Just don't look in any windows of the Big House...

LAKEHURST

NAVAL AIR STATION

Unsettled weather plagued the afternoon of May 6, 1937 at Naval Air Station Lakehurst. A cold front blew in off the Atlantic and Germany's *Hindenburg* (LZ-129), "the Titanic of airships," floated above the Navy base waiting out the thunderstorm in order to dock with its mooring mast. No one could imagine that in a few short hours 36 passengers and crew members would be dead, victims of a horrific fiery crash.

Three rapid explosions resounded. Instantly the airship became engulfed in flames. Immediately base hospital personnel flew into action and carried casualties into the branch hospital for treatment; the ambulance garage became a temporary morgue along with a section of Hangar One.

These days no one dreams of sleeping in
the clinic's basement even though comfortable
accommodations are provided for guard duty staff.
A chief petty officer making his rounds one night
wiggled a doorknob to ensure security. As he walked
away, the doorknob rattled back at him. At times,
clinic workers feel certain they are being watched.
Further eerie occurrences include lights turning
on, unexplained footsteps and loud crashes when
no other living soul is in the building. A corpsman
received the fright of his life when he observed
silver-haired woman in white floating in the air!

Another spooky spot is historic Hangar One. In the past, an airman clad in vintage fly gear greeted workers arriving for work with a hearty "Good morning!" When they do a double take, the flyboy is gone.

When The Atlantic Paranormal Society (TAPS) from the popular TV program *GhostHunters* traveled to the naval base to investigate, the then stars of the show, Jason Hawes and Grant Wilson, witnessed a figure running up one of the hangar's staircases. This entity might be the spectral navy officer observed since the time of the crash.

Electromagnetic fields are extremely high in the shelter. This could explain why people feel anxious in the area. This writer can personally attest to a feeling of terror as I left the onerous building one evening after a meeting in an upper office. I worked at Lakehurst for three years and felt an unnerving sense of unease each day as I drove onto the base.

Strangely enough, the actual *Hindenburg* crash site is the least paranormally active place on the base. Even though, they say on some evenings you can still hear hollow voices shouting "Away the lines, away the lines!" and "She's a fire!" echoing near the tarmac.

BAYVILLE

ROYAL PINES HOTEL

In 1888, Bayville's Pinewald section was known as "Barnegat Park." Initially conceived as a retirement destination for Civil War veterans, the dream faded when the economy nosedived three years later. Over time, the hotel built to house the old-timers, burned to the ground.

At an auction held in Asbury Park, New York developer Benjamin W. Sanger purchased the property. The acquisition included bay front real estate now part of the Glen Cove development. The utopian visionary imagined a luxurious resort town for wealthy urbanites. Sanger, whose wife was women's rights advocate Margaret Sanger, sold 8,000 lots between 1928 and 1929, in his "new-type, residential, recreational city-of-the sea-and-pines." Contractors started work on the already $1.2

million Royal Pines Hotel on Crystal Lake, the site of the former Barnegat Park hotel. The eight-story concrete-and-steel structure soon towered over the scrub pines.

Mystery surrounds the structure that today operates as Crystal Lake Healthcare & Rehabilitation. Rumor persists that Al Capone visited the Royal Pines Hotel. Avid *Boardwalk Empire* fans might like to imagine the Prohibition era mobster strolling about the once lavish rooms, imbibing bootlegged liquor and rolling dice at the betting tables. Some say Capone even ventured beneath the lake passing through tunnels secretly

excavated for smuggling illegal booze. But all that
is fantasy according to Lucille Glosque in *Berkeley
Township: The First 100 Years*. She writes, "Before the
hotel opened in November 1930, the stock market
crashed, signaling the Great Depression. Prohibition
ended, erasing one of the lures of the grand hotel."

As for the tunnels… Underneath the "boat
house" in front of the main building a sealed tunnel
does exist although no one knows how far it goes.
No secret stash of alcoholic spirits has ever been
unearthed yet ethereal souls show up inside the
former Royal Pines.

The apparition of a young girl in a white dress
sometimes appears at night near the overgrown
lake playing with a ball. Some claim her name is
"Gracie." Those who work the overnight shift call
the other ghost the "bell boy." No one knows how
this moniker emerged but any strange incident or
spooky noise is attributed to the spectral striped shirt
sporting guy who allegedly fell to his death from an
upper story window.

FORKED RIVER

OLD SCHOOLHOUSE MUSEUM

The Lacey Historical Society preserves artifacts and lore of the local region in the Old Schoolhouse Museum on Route 9. The school was erected in 1868 and remained in use until 1952 when a new grade school went up. Ten years later, the Lacey Historical Society formed and headquartered in the old school building where displays of tools, utensils, furniture and other mementoes of daily life are installed.Elizabeth McGrath is the vice-president of the historical society and she says something always happens when she's alone in the museum. She finds photos are moved from one place to another and the doll carriages also change position. The phone will ring and there is no one on the line. The printer goes dead for no reason and then later operates perfectly. The glass bookcase is found wide open where photos of barefoot pupils are displayed. Elizabeth believes the presence is the leftover energy of one or more former students.

These days paranormal investigators assist in validating supernatural experiences. The historical society called in the Southern Jersey Shore Paranormal Research team to evaluate the eerie situation. Elizabeth and several other museum members joined the paranormal group headed by

Lori Flurchick. It literally was a dark and stormy night when the group set up their ghost hunting equipment on, of all days, a Friday the 13th.

Operating in the dark, team members used tape recorders, motion detectors and video cameras to determine the presence of unusual energies. In one room the temperature dropped seven degrees within minutes. Elizabeth actually had goose bumps (!) as the team called out to a presence they sensed in the museum. Despite using brand new batteries in some of their equipment, the power went dead. The crystals on the chandeliers swayed back and forth. As expected, children's voices responded to questions posed by the investigators.

There's something mysterious going on in the quaint old schoolhouse museum. Check it out and be prepared to possibly experience the pupils from the past.

BARNEGAT

ELIZABETH V. EDWARDS SCHOOL

Bill Cox left his home one night at two a.m. in response to an alarm at the Barnegat Board of Education office. Just another day at the office for the former New York City policeman, that is until he left the board office and noticed the second floor of the vacant Elizabeth V. Edwards School ablaze with light.

The next day he contacted the buildings and grounds supervisor who informed him they had been doing work on that part of the building—the former cafeteria. There's no explanation for the lights because the electrical fixtures were removed due to leaky ceilings.

Closed since 2004 because of code deficiencies, the building on Route 9 is the original Barnegat High School later used as an elementary school. Long rumored to be haunted, the school is named after

Elizabeth V. Edwards a Barnegat teacher in the early years of the 20th century. She taught her first class in the one room schoolhouse once located on Birdsall Street. When the building became an elementary school a panel decided to name the school after the town's early educator. Elizabeth passed away in 1965 at the age of 91.

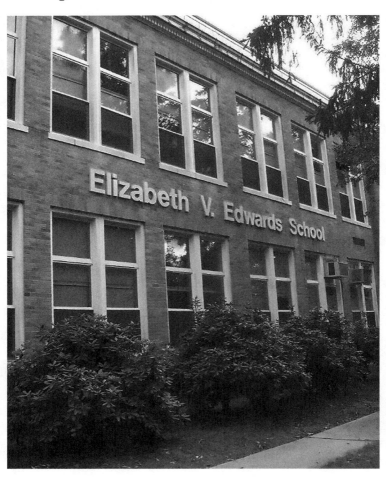

Cox is not the only staffer who experienced the inexplicable at the empty structure. As a custodian worked in the building the insistent ringing of a phone distracted him. He felt certain no phones existed in the building anymore yet he followed the sound to the principal's office and picked up a phone he saw on the desk. The phone was disconnected and without a dial tone. The same custodian also claimed he found a ladder he left in one hallway moved to another while he took a break.

Who you gonna call? Ghost busters! Susan Bové and her South Jersey Paranormal Research (SJPR) team got down to business with the tools of their trade—flashlights, electronic voice recorders, electromagnetic field detectors and digital cameras. They spent four hours in the damp and musty building where they heard inexplicable noises, music playing and audible voices. They also captured anomalous white mist in photos. One photo shows an ephemeral form sitting in a front row seat in the auditorium.

Cox says a custodian died in the basement of an apparent heart attack back in the 1970s. Is this long gone worker still on the job?

The evidence gathered by SJPR impressed the former policeman who concurs that something other worldly exists in the building.

MANAHAWKIN

WJRZ RADIO STATION

Did you know that a Jersey Shore oldies station is haunted by a ghost who loves the Beatles and Madonna? According to Susan Bové, president of the South Jersey Paranormal Research group, ghosts and spirits are attracted to music. This may be the draw for the Indian boy's spirit who haunts the broadcasting studio of WJRZ FM 100.1.

The studio sits on isolated acreage located in the coastal Pine Barrens. Leni Lenape once populated the secluded setting and it's rumored the studio is sited on an Indian burial ground. This might explain why staffers encountered the young native. On-air personalities describe childlike pranks such as settings being changed on their electronic equipment and the eerie sound of disembodied footsteps. According to staffers, the entity likes to play with knobs and cause computer glitches. Occasionally workers are so unnerved being alone they need to flee the building.

Using audio recorders, infrared cameras and hi-resolution digital photography, the South Jersey Ghost Research team investigated the site for paranormal activity. They did not encounter the youth but they did capture some interesting evidence. When one researcher felt a presence next to her, investigator Deb Thornton snapped a photo that revealed an orb. Another large orb floated in the hallway accompanied by the recording of a haunting female voice saying, "Let me out." In the kitchen, Bové recorded a male voice saying, "Turn it off" and another voice asking, "Are you filming tonight, Bill?" This cheeky remark seemed clearly aimed at Bill, WJRZ's engineer, who brought a video camera to film the investigation that night.

To listen to the EVPs go to: http://www.sjpr.org/case-studies/manahawkin-nj-october-24-2004/.

BEACH HAVEN

THE WRECKER

Several types of pirates exist—buccaneers, corsairs, privateers and many others. Each moniker may possess a slightly different meaning but the results remain the same—ill-begotten gains. Some of these scoundrels became high-seas murderers and thieves while others operated entirely on land. These land-based bandits were called "wreckers." Most operated as scavengers preying on shipwrecks— vessels driven by storms too close to the coast. The worst of these terrestrial tyrants lured ships to their doom oblivious to the fatal carnage they caused in pursuit of their spoils.

In the 18th century, one method the land pirates employed involved slowly walking with a lantern up and down the sand dunes. Visible out at sea, the wrecker wanted a ship's captain to observe the bobbing light and reason that another ship anchored in safe harbor. Supposedly as the captain steered toward the protected port his ship would run aground or wreck on treacherous shoals. The land pirates then looted and burned the hapless ship and made away with the bounty.

Despite the prevalence of the legend that some ships were deliberately lured into danger by false lights, shipping experts assert such ploys simply would not work. Perhaps the deceptions didn't work but that's not to say the ruse wasn't attempted.

One Long Beach Island visitor told me one night
as he sat on the beach enjoying the soothing rhythm
of the waves he watched a wedding celebration.
He observed the hopeful revelers from afar as
they released sky lanterns into the heavens. After
the wish lanterns floated skyward one remained
earthbound. For a long time he watched the odd
spectacle. Obviously puzzled by this event and
mildly distraught he said, "It was as if someone
was walking slowly back and forth along the beach
holding a lantern. I blinked and he was gone. Do you
have any idea what that might have been?"

I certainly do. A long-gone wrecker.

IGGITY AG

There once was an old woman who lived alone in a dilapidated house in Beach Haven. Every day she walked to town along Bay Avenue dressed in a heavy woolen coat no matter the weather. Children followed her and taunted her and called her "Iggity Ag." She never uttered a word.

Her disheveled presence on the street looks out of character in the "Queen City." Formerly, the late 19th resort catered to wealthy Philadelphians who summered at the shore in Victorian splendor.

To this day, the eccentric woman's specter is spotted downtown walking along the boulevard. Diners in local restaurants, who observe her walk by wearing her out of place attire invariably do a double take—rarely do they realize that what they see is a full-fledged apparition. Sometimes the poor soul's ghost is accompanied by disembodied, sing-song voices chanting "Iggity Ag. Iggity Ag."

TUCKERTON

J.D. THOMPSON INN

In 1823, John D. Thompson, Esquire, settled in Tuckerton. A prominent statesman and area businessman, Thompson held the position of Postmaster and also served as Sheriff of Burlington County. In 1828, he purchased the Tuckerton Stage Line. At the time, the stage carried the mail and served as the only public conveyance from Tuckerton to Philadelphia.

Thompson operated the stage line and a tavern from his homestead, today's J.D. Thompson Inn. The historic structure located on the west side of the inn served as the village post office. In 1899 George and Helen Mott took over the property which remained in the Mott family for 97 years. Jim Mott, a descendant of the second owners, explained the oldest part of the house lodged stage coach travelers overnight. Guests stayed on the first or second floor or in the third floor attic depending on what class ticket they purchased.

In 1996 the extensively renovated building became a bed and breakfast inn. Lorenzo and Catherine Lauro purchased the lodge in 2004 and continue to operate the historic Victorian B&B.

As far as ghost stories go the former stage coach stop is gently haunted. Remarkably, every year in the days leading up to Christmas, a strong smell of the sea manifests in one particular parlor room. Lauro playfully suggests it might be "Captain Bragg" coming home to visit for the holiday. (Captain Bragg was a character in the 1947 film *The Ghost and Mrs.*

Muir. The cranky sea captain's ghost tried to scare off the new owner of his house). There is no explanation for the salty scent. Since it transpires every holiday season we can conclude that *someone* comes home for Christmas.

Another oddity occurred in the old house. When Lorenzo Lauro called down to Catherine, who he thought was doing laundry in the basement, *someone* responded—but it wasn't Catherine because she wasn't in the house at the time. The question remains—*who* answered Lorenzo? That's the kind of ghost I want in my house… someone who does the laundry.

HAMMONTON

BATSTO MANSION

The Batsto Village Restoration and nearby Atsion Lake located in Wharton State Forest offer a glimpse of life in the Pine Barrens from the 1760s to the 1850s.

Charles Read is credited with building the Batsto Iron Works along the Batsto River in 1766. The area offered the natural resources necessary for making iron. Bog ore was extracted from the banks of streams and rivers, trees fueled the fires and water powered the manufacturing. The Iron Works produced household wares such as cooking pots and kettles. During the Revolutionary War, Batsto manufactured supplies for the Continental Army.

In 1784, William Richards managed the industry and erected a 32-room mansion that served generations of ironmasters.

By the mid 1800s, iron production declined and
Batsto became a glassmaking community known for
the production of windowpanes. Joseph Wharton, a
Philadelphia businessman, purchased Batsto in 1876.
Wharton continued to increase his property holdings
in the surrounding area and improved many village
buildings. His renovation of the ironmaster's
mansion transformed the structure into the elegant
Italianate manse we know today. The impressive
mansion is the centerpiece of the village and reflects
the prosperity enjoyed during Batsto's heyday.
Fourteen rooms in the Italianate-style structure,
including the parlors, dining room, library and
bedrooms, are currently open to the public.

Some visitors claim the place is haunted

according to Charles Adams III in his book *Atlantic County Ghost Stories*. He says certain sightseers observe a figure peering out the upper story windows. A few even captured a human likeness in their photos. Others allege to see lights ablaze in a third floor window of the empty mansion late at night. A handful state they felt a persistent disembodied tap on their shoulder.

During the 1930s and 40s, Elizabeth Brown Pezzuto's aunt and uncle served as caretakers at the mansion. Elizabeth recalls that when her uncle ascended the winding staircase at night, carrying an oil lamp to light his way, the lantern cast eerie, flickering shadows giving her goose bumps. Perhaps the pranks played by Elizabeth and her sisters precipitated the mansion's haunted reputation.

When the girls would hear visitors approaching the house to peek in the windows, just as sightseers do today, the sisters grabbed sofa pillows and hid under the windowsills. Then, as they listened to people's comments as they gazed through the windowpanes, the girls remained out of sight and tossed the pillows up in the air in order to give the peeping toms a good scare.

Although today's technology helps to confirm the existence of ghosts, proof is elusive at the Wharton Mansion and remains up in the air.

SMITHVILLE

HISTORIC SMITHVILLE

On April 16, 1854, as the packet ship *Powhatan* approached New York City, the vessel encountered a hurricane-like snowstorm near Long Beach Island. In one of the worst storms in New Jersey's history, the crew struggled against the powerful and dangerous currents but to no avail. Huge waves and fierce winds pummeled the *Powhatan* until the wooden schooner slammed against the Barnegat shoals. A large hole was punched in the bow and the vessel broke apart. All the passengers, who were primarily German immigrants, and crew perished; total loss of life was estimated at 311 people.

The victims washed ashore as far south as Atlantic City. Recovering the bodies was a grueling and gruesome task. Some corpses were easily retrieved while others floated into inlets, bays and creeks. Isaac and Robert Smith transported 54 cadavers on their boats to Smithville for mass burial. The bodies were stowed in Isaac's icehouse while neighborhood women fashioned burial garments and local men crafted crude coffins. As the time for burial in the old Quaker cemetery approached four of the bodies had disappeared says Tony Coppola, a co-owner of the Smithville Inn. Many feel the spirits of the missing manifest in Historic Smithville Village today.

The Smithville Inn and neighboring shops on Route 9 sit amidst the place where desperate farmers bravely battled British invaders during the American Revolution. In 1787, James Baremore constructed the original Smithville Inn as a stagecoach stop.

The tavern quickly became a popular stopover for those traveling along the King's Highway between Philadelphia and Cooper's Landing (today's Camden). At the time inns existed as a central meeting places for merchants, craftsmen and townsfolk as well.

The arrival of the railroad and improved road conditions signaled the end of the Smithville Inn by the turn of the 20th century.

Inveterate antique dealers, Fred and Ethel Noyes came upon Baremore's dilapidated tavern in 1951. Inspired by Colonial Williamsburg and Old Sturbridge Village, Ethel burned with the desire to establish a similar tourist destination. Driven by Ethel's passion, the couple collected vintage pieces and derelict structures throughout South Jersey. The buildings became shops where blacksmithing, decoy carving and other crafts were demonstrated.

Over the years the Noyes relocated many more historic buildings to the site thereby creating the Historic Towne of Smithville around the original stagecoach inn. Ethel died in 1978 and Fred passed away eight years later. The couple left behind an inviting, bucolic attraction where visitors can enjoy landscaped walkways lined with quaint lakeside shops. The *Powhatan* shipwreck victims and other departed individuals left behind their legacy here as well. Mysterious murmurings, phantom footsteps and even full-bodied apparitions are a few of the paranormal goings on at Historic Smithville.

Former employees of the Smithville Inn contend the restaurant's basement is haunted. While in the ancient burrow they felt unnerved by an invisible watchful presence. One staffer said he felt like a shadowy someone gave him a bear-hug—he never entered the storeroom again.

According to an article in the *New York Daily News*, spiritual consultant and paranormal investigator Nina Circone, feels many tragic deaths are associated with the transplanted structures. For instance, in the Smithville Bakery she discerned the earthbound presence of young girls who perished in a fire. In the old firehouse, psychic medium, Lisa Wolff, channeled the spirits of two males and a little girl.

Donna Riegel is the owner of the Evermore Herb Co. One night as she entered her shop after hours she heard a woman crying. Thinking it was an employee who fell or injured herself she raced to help only there was nobody there. In fact the mystified proprietor found no living soul in the shop.

Although most of spirits are of the Colonial era, the village's ghostly population corresponds to the layers of history characteristic of the site.

Amy S. Rosenberg writes the "Downashore" blog for www.philly.com. She and her husband experienced an odd encounter in 1997 when a fire broke out in Smithville.

As fire consumed an old barn on the corner of Route 9 and Moss Mill Road, Rosenberg and her then boyfriend turned away from the sad spectacle. An older woman dressed in a stylish gown stood nearby. She stared straight ahead and stated: "That's the old Freehold Barn… what a shame." Rosenberg said the woman "…glowed in the firelight. And she took a long drag from a cigarette holder with the kind of imperiousness that once made smoking seem so glamorous. She had a gap between her two front teeth." Rosenberg and her friend glanced back at the fire then turned to say something to the woman but she had vanished.

Months later, the couple dined at Fred & Ethel's restaurant (named after the Noyes) and noticed Ethel Noyes' photo on the wall. Ethel's image exhibited a gap-toothed smile and wore a gown like the one worn by the woman who appeared at the fire. Undoubtedly, Ethel's passion for her historic village continues to this day as expressed by her uncanny appearance.

MAYS LANDING

THE ABBOTT HOUSE

Legend says the spirit of a young girl inhabits the
top floor of the Victorian designed Abbott House.
The grand home, built in the 1860s by attorney
Joseph E. P. Abbott and his wife Adeline, is situated

on Main Street two doors down from a funeral parlor and diagonally across from the First United Methodist Church graveyard. Over the years rumors persisted that the old house was haunted.

A while back, Dave Juliano, founder of the South Jersey Ghost Research (SJGR) group, received a call from the owner after she experienced unexplained activity in the home. Residents and visitors complained of hearing the sound of a bouncing ball upstairs along with mysterious creaking doors. The ghost hunting team went to work and set up their sophisticated equipment in an upstairs bedroom. Remarkably their investigation illuminated the lore attached to the house. They encountered a little girl along with the noise of a bouncing ball, according to Juliano whose team possessed no knowledge of the particulars of the haunting prior to their visit.

The team captured four electronic voice phenomena (EVP) on audiotape. EVPs are voices inaudible at the time of recording yet surface by an unknown process during playback analysis. Paranormal researchers contend these eerie recordings are the voices of the dead.

Using infrared video cameras, which are capable of filtering light rays outside of the usual visible spectrum, the team also caught roving balls of light, invisible to the naked eye. The digital camera revealed the light orbs as well. These light globules are generally thought to hold spirit energy.

According to psychics, another disembodied resident is a 16-year-old boy dubbed "David." The mediums attribute the haunting to the young man's trauma of being locked inside a closet as punishment when he was alive. As a consequence of this abuse, his spirit remains trapped due to his emotional and physical mistreatment.

In the past the young man's spirit appeared to certain children but mostly he stayed hidden *opening and closing doors* to announce his presence.

ATLANTIC COUNTY COURTHOUSE

In addition to fulfilling the duties of their job descriptions, Atlantic County Courthouse staffers have to contend with the paranormal. The halls of justice jingle with the sound of clanking keys and jiggling doorknobs. Elevators, light fixtures and water faucets seem to have a mind of their own in the 1883 building. Ghostly sobs fill Courtroom No. 1, the oldest courtroom in the building . Many hear a woman crying in the chamber but when they check, nobody's there.

Jo DiStephano Kapus, a past president of the Atlantic County Historical Society and a former title searcher who worked many years in the courthouse, diligently researched the mysterious manifestations at the county seat at 5909 Main Street. She traces the otherworldly occurrences to real-life incidents.

Kapus unearthed a local newspaper story from 1898 recounting a saga about a missing ten-year-old boy, Japheth Connolly. Two days later, his strangled body turned up in a shallow grave near Somers Point. The ensuing investigation yielded evidence linking William O'Mara to the crime.

During the trial, O'Mara's and Japheth's mothers wept profusely throughout the entire proceeding. Found guilty, O'Mara escaped lynching but received a 25 year sentence of hard labor. Did the energy of these grieving women leave its imprint upon the courtroom? Some feel certain because when a former senior court clerk and two other employees heard unmistakable sobbing emanating from the back of the courtroom they witnessed a vaporous form shaped like a human being.

Once as a judge held court in the room he asked the bailiff to go upstairs and corral the child who ran back and forth. The officer didn't discover any children in the entire building. Other witnesses report the scampering sound in the upstairs corridors. Could this be Japheth Connolly's spirit?

During the 19th century executions used to take place at the "hanging tree" in front of the courthouse. Some onlookers watching the grisly scene became hysterical. Do the spirits of those lynched on the property or witnesses to their slaying still linger here?

Several feel another ghostly perpetrator may be the man who in 1950 hanged himself in the bell tower. Others think a former inmate who died of a heart attack while attempting to crack open a safe is one of the creepy culprits.

Poltergeist activity is also prevalent. In the break room an officer observed a soup ladle fly from the table and land in front of the microwave oven. Then the dish holding the spoon flipped upside down right before his eyes.

The historic trauma generated here has produced a paranormal ferment that rivals few other haunted places along the Jersey Shore.

ATLANTIC CITY

RESORTS CASINO HOTEL

In 1850, Absecon Island resident, Dr. Jonathan Pitney, imagined an ideal health retreat in the area. The visionary brought the first railroad to the island and created today's street grid pattern. Pitney named his Atlantic City streets running parallel to the Atlantic after the oceans and the streets running east to west after the states. When the first train pulled into the station from Camden in 1854, the tourists disembarked in droves.

Real estate developers soon recognized Atlantic City's potential as a resort destination. Before Resorts International formed, two three-story wooden Quaker rooming houses, the Chalfonte House (1868) and the Haddon House (1869) stood on the site. In 1900, Henry Leeds purchased the Chalfonte House property and constructed an eight-story iron-frame and brick-face "skyscraper" which opened its doors to guests in 1904 as the Chalfonte Hotel.

The current Haddon Hall building was constructed in stages in the 1920s. The 11-story wing facing the Boardwalk was constructed first, with the 15-story center and 11-story rear wings added later in the decade. Soon after its completion Haddon Hall merged with the adjacent Chalfonte via a skyway, which still exists today. Almost immediately ghostly rumors began to swirl. The upper floors of the thousand room hotel were freezing according to guests who felt the chilly atmosphere signaled the presence of ghosts. The brick and steel building swayed with the wind which howled through the halls adding to the haunted reputation.

The Chalfonte-Haddon Hall played a vital role during World War II when Atlantic City beaches were used for manoeuvres and armed forces training at "Camp Boardwalk." Haddon Hall transformed into Thomas England General Hospital for wounded soldiers.

In Resorts' Ocean Tower, a feature of the original Haddon Hall and the oldest part of the property, a few people have experienced the paranormal as claimed by a hotel representative. A couple from North Carolina felt uncomfortable during their stay according to a review on Trip Advisor (tripadvisor.

com). The woman wrote, "My husband and I stayed in the Ocean Tower and the whole time we were there it felt like someone or something was in the room with us. The sixth floor hallway just felt so creepy like someone died there. We kept hearing bumping and the door would shake." Thinking other guests cavorted in the hall she opened the door and found no one.

In fact several individuals did transpire there. Hundreds of soldiers billeted in the Chalfonte-Haddon Hall Hotel building during WWII and many expired from illness and their injuries.

Apparitions of corpsmen walk the hallways and hotel-registration areas according to some. Could the appearance of the eerie soldiers account for the supernatural experiences reported by guests?

Former Resorts employees who used to take their smoking breaks in the basement, which served as the temporary hospital morgue, described it as "kind of creepy." Resorts claims the on-site morgue was actually on the 12th floor but the basement location seems more logical due to cooler temperatures. Just knowing that a morgue existed on-site is enough to give one the willies!

Unlike most other hotels, Resorts designates a 13th floor. Due to superstition of something sinister associated with the number 13, it's commonplace for hotel management not to allow a 13th floor. Resorts, however, brazenly houses its Piano Bar and the Pro Bar dance club on number 13.

Curiously, another Resorts team member who is sensitive to spirits, shared that "As a new Resorts' employee I attended the required orientation meeting. During the course of training, the head of security took our group on a tour of the building. We rode the elevator to the 13th floor which at the time was the VIP Club. When I exited the elevator I suddenly felt surrounded by a mob of spirits—I mean a lot of spirits. It was like being in a crowd of hundreds. I couldn't understand why there were so many spirits roaming and swirling around me. We continued our tour and when finished, returned to the orientation room. Our guide told us that during World War II the hotel was used as a hospital and that the 13th floor was where the operating rooms were located. To me, that explained why there were so many spirits still wandering the corridors."

A feral cat colony exists under the boardwalk outside Resorts. Frank Scoblete in his article "The Ghosts of Atlantic City's Resorts Hotel" published in the *Casino City Times*, states that on some early mornings, a spectral woman in black walks the beach. A multitude of mewing felines announces her arrival as her specter goes about feeding and tending to the homeless cats.

He goes on to say ethereal nurses push ghostly carriages and wheel chairs and are seen assisting phantom children outside the hotel particularly in the vicinity of the valet parking. After a while they slowly fade from view.

Think twice if you spot a Charlie Chaplin type character inside the casino. This personality is a revenant from the past so give him a nod as he tips his hat in greeting.

OCEAN CITY

CITY HALL

In 1879 four Methodist ministers chose the barrier island as a suitable spot to establish a Christian retreat. They chose to name their settlement "Ocean City," laid out streets and sold lots for cottages, hotels and businesses.

City Hall is situated in the heart of the downtown area at 9th Street and Asbury Avenue. The imposing building was built in 1914 and added to the National Registry of Historic Places in 1997. The Mayor's office and other municipal departments are housed within the edifice. Harry Headley was the first mayor to occupy the impressive building thought a reckless expenditure at the time. Headley spent his entire career in service to the Ocean City community. He enjoyed many terms as mayor as well as councilman and established the police and fire departments in addition to the library.

Today there are many who feel this pillar of the community continues serving his constituents in subtle ways. Opening doors, disembodied footsteps and an unpredictable elevator are some haunting hallmarks attributed to the former mayor. One night a custodian encountered an older, well-dressed man in the vicinity of the Council Chambers. The petrified custodian stood immobilized as the wraith walked right through him!

Several administrators working late into the night heard the distinctive sound of the elevator moving between floors then the sound of footsteps down the hall and through the double doors. When they investigated no one was found.

City Public Relations Director Mark Soifer says the spirit is believed to be former treasurer, Anthony Imbesi. Soifer worked with Imbesi and describes him as "a warm, kindly person who really loved his job." He says "If it is Mr. Imbesi, City Hall couldn't have a nicer ghost."

OCEAN VIEW

SEAVILLE TAVERN

Although many "spirited" sites are historic and possess a history of habitation this is not always the case. On-site death or trauma is not a prerequisite for a haunted place. Spirits can decide to return to their favorite environment out of habit or for comfort. This appears to be the motive for the spirits drawn to the Seaville Tavern. Constructed in 1976 on an unimproved piece of property unattached to any remarkable events, the packaged goods store and deli eventually grew into today's popular landmark pub.

Diane Hogan, the tavern manager, served up some haunting tales. She related her cook Gina felt a hand on her back while preparing food. "This is something that we do, when we want to make sure that they don't back up and get hurt." The phantom seems focused in the galley where disembodied kitchen noises, like someone using pots and pans and dishes and utensils are common. One night at closing, server Daria Adams and Gerry Chretien heard footsteps in the restaurant. They walked around the entire establishment but found no one.

Liz Oldenburger and Jennifer Teets both sighted furtive figures in their peripheral vision. In fact, one day as Diane walked into the restaurant her server Aimee Wynne seemed surprised and asked, "Where did you just come from?" Diane replied she came from the liquor store. Aimee wondered because she observed someone walk towards the front door. These spooky incidents add a curious element to the friendly tavern.

The most dramatic spirit manifestation appeared in a photo snapped by a bar patron. With his cell phone he inadvertently captured the image of a cloudy human figure that appears to be standing on the bar. Some regulars now use a "ghost app" to detect spirits in the eatery and when they do the device "goes crazy."

The Seaville Tavern's atmosphere and food are crazy good—these creature comforts provide a favored haunt for locals and those not of this world.

WILDWOOD, BY THE SEA

GEORGE F. BOYER MUSEUM

The structure at 3907 Pacific Avenue housing the George F. Boyer Museum was originally Ingersoll's Funeral Home. Chilling enough, but in consequence of many unexplainable happenings transpiring in the building, the Cumberland County Paranormal organization came to investigate the anomalies.

Some of the unusual claims made by museum volunteers include unexplainable smoke scents and sweet smells. Fire was ruled out although Wildwood has seen its share. The museum contains a mix of boardwalk memorabilia. Could the old artifacts exude an aroma of days gone by? During their inspection, the Cumberland ghost hunters caught a whiff of pipe tobacco. In all cases the smells suddenly surfaced then disappeared just as quickly.

Museum docents reported that on several occasions when they answered the ringing telephone no one was on the line. Crank caller or paranormal prankster? Also, the security alarm sounded in the middle of the night without cause. Motion sensor lights went off yet quickly returned to normal. This is odd because when the motion sensor is activated, the light is set to stay lit for a certain period before blinking off. One volunteer stated he opened the building one morning to find the motion sensor activated signaling movement inside.

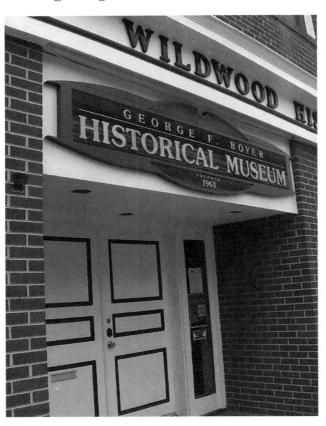

The night of the paranormal investigation all of the Cumberland researchers distinctly felt they were being watched. A palpable presence gave an aura of "reserved curiosity" to quote lead investigator, Clay Borneman. He said, "The best way to describe it is the feeling of being observed by a curious child told not to talk to strangers." He sensed the presence kept "peeking around corners to see what the new people were doing."

The group captured compelling electronic voice phenomena that warrant a follow up investigation. When asked "Do you like it here?" a garbled response was recorded. A second recording also contains indistinguishable sounds by an entity seemingly eager to communicate.

Borneman and his group believe "the energies inhabiting a location need to feel as comfortable with us as researchers as we do with them as residents. Often, the first research event is merely an introduction and sometimes it takes several events for the residents to become comfortable enough with us to really 'come out of their shell,' so-to-speak." We'll have to wait and see if Borneman and his group can coax the spirits to the surface during future investigations.

J. THOMPSON BAKER HOUSE

The J. Thompson Baker National Historic House, at 3008 Atlantic Avenue, is named after its former owner, a New Jersey congressman and one of three brothers who founded and developed the Wildwoods. Built in 1904, President Woodrow Wilson stayed at the historic house during a campaign junket six days before his 1912 election.

Baker was Wildwood's first mayor and his former dwelling is now home to the Wildwood Civic Club. The interior décor is reminiscent of life during Baker's residency. Books of the era as well as children's toys lie scattered throughout as if the residents still inhabited their home. There are those who feel some family members do stay behind.

Some civic club members avoid going into the building by themselves after dark even though they can't say exactly why— *something* inside causes a feeling of unease. Some visitors to the residence heard footsteps in the foyer and on the front porch. When they looked to see who came in no one was there.

The strange goings-on prompted Theresa Williams, president of the Friends of the J. Thompson Baker House, to welcome the Cumberland County

Paranormal research group. The team of ghost hunters, headed by Clay Borneman, captured a number of electronic voice phenomena. The group recorded indistinguishable voices while taping on the main staircase and also taped strange noises in the attic. A journalist reporting on the paranormal investigation observed a couple dressed in vintage clothing in his peripheral vision.

The civic club conducts historic house tours, a worthwhile expedition, and various other events throughout the year. Pay a visit to the home and see what shows up in *your* line of vision...

CAPE MAY

HISTORIC COLD SPRING VILLAGE

Historic Cold Spring Village is a living history museum portraying daily life of a rural South Jersey community. From late June to early September, interpreters and artisans, wearing Early American period clothing, preserve the trades, crafts and heritage of a simpler time by demonstrating basket weaving, woodworking, blacksmithing, pottery making and other skills.

In addition to experiencing the village's 26 restored, historic buildings dating from 1691–1912, guests are offered a number of workshops and demonstrations. The village is the perfect venue for the programs highlighting spiritualism and the paranormal because for decades, village workers and visitors have sighted the spirit of an American Indian. His stately form appears dressed in buckskin as he prowls the property's outer limits. Originally, Leni-Lenape Indians inhabited this region of New Jersey so his presence is consistent with history. But his is not the only apparition native to the village.

At times an almost eerie ambiance pervades the little community; the atmosphere thick with spirits from the past. The relocated buildings in the enclave, constructed over a period of two centuries, exude a lot of energy. On my first visit, I encountered Phil Calfina, a long-time village caretaker. "See that building over there?" he said, pointing toward the Dennisville Inn. "I see three ladies wearing shawls walking out of there nearly every night." "Real women?" I asked him. "No! Ghosts!"

Built in 1836 and originally located on Main
Street in Dennisville, the Federal style building
operated as a tavern and inn on the Philadelphia
to Cape May stage route. Back in the day taverns
served as centers for town meetings and social
gatherings as well as a lodging place for stagecoach
travelers. In 1870, a Baptist owner acquired the
property where he conducted church assemblies
and meetings. The building features two front
doors—one opens into the center hall and the other
into the bar room. It feels right that the three female
apparitions are leftover energy from the Baptist
era yet they exit from the tavern door. Nineteenth
century women were prohibited in bars so now that

these ladies inhabit the afterlife perhaps they are free to imbibe.

Calfina stated spirits exists all over the village. "I see them everywhere," he said. Calfina is not the only employee with extrasensory vision. Other staff members affirm the village is home to numerous spirits.

The charming Greek revival style Ewing-Douglass House accommodates the Ice Cream Parlor. Most likely farmer David Ewing built the house around 1850. In 1869, Nathaniel Douglass acquired the property and ran a country store in a side addition since removed. The ghostly occupant here is a petite woman who when she appears is holding a lit candle as if standing vigil for a loved one.

Tammy Patterson interprets a 19th century housewife by demonstrating open-hearth cooking and gardening. While tending to her duties Tammy experienced a fright in the Spicer Leaming House. Built around 1820 on land now submerged under the Cape May Canal, the farmhouse was home to Colonel Jacob Spicer, a 17th century settler, and his subsequent descendants, the Leamings. In 1750, his son Jacob Spicer Esq. along with Aaron Leaming, published the "Concessions & Agreements," establishing freedom of religion, freedom of speech, trial by jury, elections and other rights for New Jersey citizens. Oddly, the ghost in residence is not related to the house's history.

Patterson relates that as she returned to the house one day after fetching water, she noticed a young girl staring out a second-story window. Patterson thought the girl might be an apprentice assigned to assist. She smiled at the girl who smiled back. Patterson entered the Spicer Leaming home went upstairs to welcome the girl but found no one there. Patterson's fright nearly caused her to quit her job. Fortunately for Patterson, she only sighted the apparition one time but the girl ghost remains. The interpreter feels the phantom tug on her clothes, she opens and shuts doors and she enjoys relaxing in the rocking chair. Patterson claims the young spirit seems to linger upstairs by a doll bed.

The story took an even more inexplicable turn during the following season when a couple, who heard of Patterson's experience in the house, asked her to share her story with them. When she complied the man started to cry. He revealed that he donated the doll bed to the village when his 10-year-old daughter passed away; the crib was her favorite toy.

CAPE MAY PUFFIN SUITES

In the 1600s, Native Americans traveled a sandy trail
to the sea that eventually developed into today's
Jackson Street where beautiful homes and inns
line the timeworn path. Jackson Street is also Cape
May's most haunted avenue. Psychic medium Craig
McManus suggests this location may be an energy
vortex that draws and holds spirits. The Cape May
Puffin Suites at 32 Jackson Street is a case in point.

The South Jersey Ghost Research (SJGR) group
originated in 1955. Currently the organization
consists of 30 volunteer members who participate in

weekly paranormal investigations and educational outreach. Dave Juliano directs the ghost hunting team who set off to explore the haunted house.

The psychic investigators perceived several spirits in the building. In the Terrace Suite, two team members received impressions of timid immigrants who once lived downstairs. Several sensed the presence of a man in the Holly Suite and in the second floor hallway. In the Main Quarters Suite, particularly in the front bedroom, the presence of a different man was felt, a dyed-in-the-wool chauvinist. Fifteen positive EMF (electric magnetic field) readings indicated a spirit presence along with four EVP (electronic voice phenomena) recordings.

While surveying the Main Quarters Suite, researcher Tim Becker sensed an entity who seemed annoyed that strangers were present in his house without his permission. When co-investigator Kathy Dougherty complained of a pain in her neck, Tim observed a bright orb fly past her. Orbs are considered an indication of a spirit presence. Then he observed a dark figure walk past the window leading to the porch. When he investigated he found no one. Tim suspects the male energy is a bad-tempered, misogynistic and possessive individual—the king of the castle—no wonder this spirit occupies the Main Quarters Suite.

In the Terrace Suite, when investigator Brian Jenkins felt a presence he asked the spirit to share things about himself. He continued to address the phantom in a conversational way for over a minute and finally finished by imploring "tell me anything." A man's voice says "I'm frightened by you." I guess some ghosts are as frightened by us as some of us are by them. In the Holly Suite while audio recording for EVPs, Brian got the distinct feeling he was not alone. He said, "I know somebody's here, who are you?" A man's voice says "Hello?"

The photos of orbs and the electromagnetic field anomalies at this B&B is sufficient reason to suspect spirit energies lodge here. Brian assessed the energies as *residual* rather than conscious spirit presences—simply imprinted energy fields rooted in some traumatic incident that transpired at the location. A residual haunting is a playback of a past event where the spirit is oblivious to the living. When a spirit entity interacts with the living it's termed an "intelligent" haunting.

Cape May Puffin Suites offer a warm and welcoming atmosphere where the spirits who inhabit the home are benign characters living out the past.

CAPE MAY FISH MARKET

When Paula Geserick first entered the building that houses the Cape May Fish Market she knew right away the building was special. As it turns out the Washington Street Mall location is extraordinary because the spot is a hotbed of paranormal activity harboring at least eight (!) ghosts.

Michael and Steven Slawek purchased the property and established the restaurant seven years ago. Installed as general manager, Paula thoroughly savors her role but finds the quiet time after hours most enticing. Although comfortable being alone in the eatery after closing, the atmosphere felt different one night as she stayed to catch up with work. Paula suspected she was being watched so she surveyed the room and spotted a man who looked a lot like Abraham Lincoln. Paula dashed out of the building.

Even though Paula is used to seeing ghosts, she sighted her first apparition at 11-years-old, being face to face with a specter is nevertheless unnerving. She particularly took exception when the same Lincoln-like ghost showed up in her bedroom. That's when she called in ghost buster Craig McManus.

The psychic medium has yet to fully investigate the restaurant but when he walked through he sensed the presence of at least eight spirits. He says the location is a gathering place of sorts for entities with no place else to go. He also felt the building may have functioned as a brothel. This presumption aligns with Paula's sighting of an older, plump woman with gray hair severely styled in a bun. The gray woman exudes an imposing presence and most likely served as the "house mother" or madam.

Full-bodied apparitions are one of the most dramatic manifestations of the afterlife but they are only the beginning of the goings-on at the Cape May Fish Market. One waitress had her pony tail pulled others observed pictures fall off the wall—one at a time. On one occasion, Paula hung her sweater on a clothes hook and for some reason, looked back at the sweater. Inexplicably the arm stood straight out then flopped down—as if an unseen hand held it out then let go. This anomaly occurred in front of two witnesses.

When the South Jersey Ghost Research (SJGR) organization surveyed the eatery they experienced the energy of a black man in the kitchen who psychics identified as the house steward. His spirit stays behind performing chores and preparing meals. Other perceived phantoms are women outfitted in typical Victorian attire, large hats and long dresses, and men in suits.

The spirits haunting the CM Fish Market actively responded to questions asked by investigators via thumping noises and causing the Tri-Field meter to react (the Tri-Field meter is a device used to measure electromagnetic fields).

Physical anomalies transpired during SJGR's investigation as well. Two researchers experienced a temperature drop of 8 degrees in less than a minute and one felt something brush up against her right arm. Two investigators reported seeing shadows while investigating the basement. Another heard a voice and what sounded like footsteps coming from the back of the room and reported the chair next to her moved.

In an attempt to interact with the spirits and gain specific information about the resident entities, investigators ask questions utilizing the REM pod, a device used to detect energy disturbances and fluctuations. The occupant spirits here caused the REM to alarm repeatedly in response to questions posed. During a particular EVP session utilizing the REM pod an investigator received the impression of a female spirit with long blonde hair wearing a blue dress. Investigator Bridget LeConey asks, "Did you have a blue dress?" The REM responds affirmatively. Then, "Do you like the changes happening upstairs?" REM lights up. "Would you like to see people living there when it's fixed up?" REM lights up again. Another investigator then telepathically "hears" the female entity say, "Yeah, then I could borrow their clothes." Paula laughed remembering the episode with her sweater. Bridget asked, "Do you like Paula's sweaters?" REM immediately lit up.

Some clairvoyants discern an adverse aspect; the structure has certainly seen its share of sadness, loss and violence. A lot of lingering energy exists throughout the building but SJGR picked up particularly strong energies in the second and third floor restrooms. Paula herself experienced a disembodied woman in the second floor restroom. The spirits sensed emit deep sadness—one in relation to her loss of a loved one, the other over her fate as a prostitute. Investigators also picked up impressions of both suicide and murder in the building. The violence is associated with prostitution, gambling and drug use that occurred throughout the building's history. One said, "…the energy feels residual but there are many layers. I believe the apartments were used as a boarding house for blue collar workers and this eventually degenerated into a low-rent complex filled with drugs, prostitution and gambling. There were constant fights, yelling and violence."

Although the history of the 1868 building is sketchy many different people have passed through its portals over the course of nearly 150 years. Strong emotions generated here have created a lasting impression on 408 Washington Street that continues to manifest in a myriad of mysterious ways.

In Closing...

THE LINDA LEE

In *Haunted Cape May* I resisted the urge to write about The Linda Lee, a haunted Victorian B&B among many in Cape May. An obvious choice as we share the same name although spelled differently. For this volume of ghost stories I succumb because sadly, the guesthouse on Columbia Avenue closed and I feel sorry for the ephemeral residents who may be lonely for a little while... not forevermore I hope.

When psychic medium Craig McManus tried to communicate with the resident ghosts at a nearby location he drew the attention of Walter, a pleasant, older man who lived across the street at 725 Columbia Avenue, the former Linda Lee. In an article written for the CapeMay.com blog, McManus states, "Walter waltzed in through the front wall and announced his arrival. He told me his name was Walter and he came because he enjoyed good wine and good cheese and none was being served across the street where he was haunting." A spirit after my own heart!

The Benezets were merchants in town who built the Victorian Carpenter Gothic in 1872. Only a whisper of haunting activity existed which explains my reticence to chronicle this particular haunted B&B. Disembodied footsteps were the only tell-tale sign of Walter's presence. (Although that's pretty creepy). Psychic impressions received by McManus revealed Walter formerly owned the property and passed away in the house. He also unearthed another long-gone occupant. A woman named Mary.

According to the medium, Mary, an apparent maid from the Benezet era, seemed weary of keeping house. I'd be too after more than a century of scrubbing. Mary possesses a strong connection to the dwelling because she loved the place. I love it too.

So it's goodbye for now to The Linda Lee and to you dear reader. Until next time… Happy Hauntings!

"Celestial matters do not easily lend themselves
to terrestrial thinking and logic."
~ Michael Tymn

GHOST TOURS
OF THE JERSEY SHORE

Jersey Shore Ghost Tours
(www.jerseyshoreghosttours.com)

Asbury Park's Ghosts and Legends Tours
(www.paranormalbooksnj.com)

Into the Mystic Ghost and Legend Walking Tour
(www.lunasea32@gmail.com)

Ghosts & Legends of Historic Smithville Village
Green (www.paranormalbooksnj.com)

Absecon Lighthouse Ghost Tours
(www.abseconlighthouse.org)

Ghost Tour of Ocean City
(www.ghosttour.com)

Elaine's (Cape May) Ghost Tours
(www.elainesdinnertheater.com)

Ghosts of Cape May and
Ghosts of the Lighthouse Trolley Tours
(www.capemaymac.org)

BE SURE TO VISIT...

ACKNOWLEDGEMENTS

I want to express my sincere appreciation to the following individuals who generously and graciously contributed their time and information:

Boni Bates, Founder
Garden State Ghost Hunters

Clay Borneman, Co-founder & Director
Cumberland County Paranormal

Tina Kush Crepezzi

Danny & Pamela A. Garber

Paula Geserick, General Manager
Cape May Fish Market

Diane Hogan, Manager
Elizabeth Oldenburger
Jennifer Teets
Seaville Tavern

Dave Juliano, Founder
Bridget LeConey, Assistant Director
South Jersey Ghost Research

Linda Keating

Kathy A. Kelly, Founder
Paranormal Museum

Gloria C. Kudrick, Case Manager/Investigator
Behind the Wall Paranormal Research

Catherine Lauro, Co-Owner
J.D. Thompson Inn

Elizabeth McGrath, Vice-President
Lacey Township Historical Society

Donna Riegel
Evermore Herb Co.

Joanne Weithenauer, D.V.M.

Theresa Williams, President
Friends of the J. Thompson Baker House

Many thanks to my partners in publishing:
Deb Tremper, Graphic Designer
Six Penny Graphics
&
The Staff at Sheridan Books, Inc.

I would especially like to thank my friends Susan
Grahn and Maryann Way for their unfailing
advice, enthusiasm, insight and support.

I particularly appreciate all my readers!
Your enthusiasm and support inspire my research
and keep me chronicling haunted history.

BIBLIOGRAPHY

Adams, Charles J. III. *Atlantic County Ghost Stories*. Exeter House
    Books, 2003.

"Al Capone and the Royal Pines Hotel." Retrieved from
    http://weirdnj.com/stories/al-capone-royal-pines-hotel.

Anonymous. "Shipwrecked Ghosts in the Basement of the
    Smithville Inn." *Weird NJ*, Volume #19, 2002.

Bergen, Douglas. "Haunted House." Ocean City Patch.
    October 22, 2012.

"Caretakers Ponder Spooky Occurrence." *Reading Eagle*, July 2, 1978.

Cox, Bill. "Recalling a Historic Barnegat Resident."
    Barnegat-Manahawkin Patch, October 26, 2013.

Davis, Eddie. "Five Really Haunted Places in South Jersey."
    LiteRock 96.9 FM, October 22, 2013.

Fact or Faked, Paranormal Files (SyFy channel). "Bay Area Hysteria/
    Jersey Shore Haunting." Season 2, Episode 14, April 24, 2012.

Glosque, Lucille. *Berkeley Township: The First 100 Years*.
    Berkeley Township Centennial Commission, 1975.

Hopkins, Amanda. "Ghost Stories: Voices from Beyond."
    Atlantic City Weekly, October 10, 2012.

_____. "Cold Springs Ghosts." *Atlantic City Weekly*, October 17, 2012.

_____. "Spirits Lingers at Resorts." *Atlantic City Weekly*,
    October 24, 2012.

Kelly, Kathy A. *Asbury Park's Ghosts and Legends*. Paranormal Books &
    Curiosities Publishing, 2010.

Kimmel, Richard J. and Timper, Karen E. *Folklore of the Jersey Shore*.
    Schiffer Books, 2012.

Linderoth, Matthew. *Prohibition on the North Jersey Shore*.
    History Press, 2010.

Macken, Lynda Lee. *Ghosts of the Garden State.* Black Cat Press, 2001.

_____. *Ghosts of the Garden State II.* Black Cat Press, 2003.

_____. *Ghosts of the Garden State III.* Black Cat Press, 2005.

_____. *Haunted Cape May.* Black Cat Press, 2002.

_____. *Haunted Long Beach Island.* Black Cat Press, 2013.

McManus, Craig. *Ghosts of Cape May, Book 3.* ChannelCraig, 2008.

Miller, Patricia A. "A Haunting in Barnegat?" Berkeley Patch, September 30, 2013.

_____. "Spirits Still Roam The Halls Of Old Elizabeth V. Edwards School In Barnegat." Barnegat-Manahawkin Patch, October 22, 2013.

Moran, Mark & Sceurman, Mark. *Weird N.J. Your Travel Guide to New Jersey's Local Legends and Best Kept Secrets.* Sterling Publishing, 2009.

Puglisi, Jeremy. "Oldies station is spooked." *The Times-Beacon,* October 28, 2004.

Rauber, Al. "Haunted Houses." Retrieved from http://www.scaryplace.com/HauntedAllaireVillage.html.

Reeser, A. L. *Ghost Stories of Atlantic City.* 1stSight Press, 2010.

Reeser, Tim. *Ghost Stories of Ocean City, NJ.* Ghostlore, Inc., 2003.

Roberts, Christine. "Paranormal investigators speak to the undead residents of the town of Historic Smithville, N.J." *New York Daily News,* October 16, 2012.

Rose, Elaine, "Courting Ghosts?" *The Atlantic City Press,* Atlantic City, NJ; October 31, 1992.

Rosenberg, Amy S. "The enigmatic couple who created Smithville." www.philly.com, September 18, 2013.

Shad, Jacob Jr. "Spooky Night at the Wildwood Museum." *Shore News Today,* July 7, 2011.

Scoblete, Frank. "The Ghosts of Atlantic City's Resorts Hotel." *Casino City Times*, February 25, 2010.

Staab, Amanda. "A Haunting Encounter: When Ghosts Berate The Unsuspecting." *New Jersey Monthly*, September 12, 2012.

Stetser, Laura. "Boo! There are ghosts galore in South Jersey, say paranormal researchers." *Ocean City Gazette*, October 27, 2010.

Stowinsky, Russell. "Did Al Capone Hide Out in the Royal Pines Hotel?" Berkeley Patch, July 13, 2011.

Suit, Lauren. "J. Thompson Baker house a 'hot spot' for paranormal investigators." *Shore News Today*, December 14, 2011.

Tanous, Alex & Cooper, Callum E. *Conversations with Ghosts.* White Crow Books, 2013.

The Haunting of… Eric Mabius. Season 1, Episode 2. Biography Channel, November 3, 2012.

Vosseller, Bob. "Paranormalists investigate Lacey Schoolhouse Museum." *Asbury Park Press*, June 3, 2010.

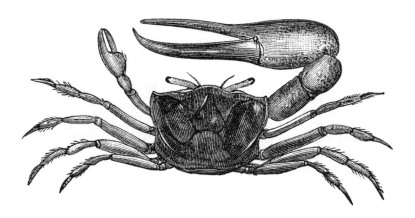

WEBSITES

Batsto Village: www.batstovillage.org

City of Cape May: www.capemaycity.com

ClipArt ETC: http://etc.usf.edu/clipart

Cumberland County Paranormal:
www.cumberlandcountyparanormal.com

Garden State Ghost Hunters: www.gardenstateghosthunters.com

Historic Cold Spring Village: www.hcsv.org

The Historic Village at Allaire: www.allairevillage.org

History of Tuckerton: www.tuckerton.com/tuckerton-history.htm

National Park Service: www.cr.nps.gov/history/online_books/nj1

NJ Pine Barrens: www.njpinebarrens.com

Ocean County Paranormal/WOBM.com NJ 101.5:
www.wobm.com/tags/ocean-county-paranormal

Resorts Casino Hotel: www.resortsac.com/history

Historic Smithville: www.smithvillenj.com

South Jersey Paranormal Research: www.sjpr.org

Southern Jersey Shore Paranormal Research:
southernjerseyshore-paranormal.com

Wall Township: www.wallnj.com

The White Lilac Inn: www.whitelilac.com

Wikipedia: www.wikipedia.org

Other Haunted Titles by
Lynda Lee Macken

Adirondack Ghosts

Adirondack Ghosts II

Adirondack Ghosts III

Array of Hope, An Afterlife Journal

Empire Ghosts, New York State's Haunted Landmarks

Ghost Hunting the Mohawk Valley

Ghostly Gotham, Haunted History of New York City

*Ghosts of Central New York

Ghosts of the Garden State

Ghosts of the Garden State II

Ghosts of the Garden State III

Ghosts of the Jersey Shore

Haunted Baltimore

Haunted Cape May

Haunted History of Staten Island

Haunted Houses of the Hudson Valley

Haunted Lake George

Haunted Long Beach Island

Haunted Long Island

Haunted Long Island II

Haunted New Hope

Haunted Salem & Beyond

*(originally published as *Leatherstocking Ghosts*)

"For those who believe, no proof is necessary.
For those who don't believe, no proof is possible."
~ Stuart Chase

Visit Lynda Lee Macken's website
www.lyndaleemacken.com